HEY, WALL

To street artists everywhere: thank you for your creativity,
bravery, activism, and ability to start a conversation

—S. V.

To "Big C," Christopher John Alteri

—J. P.

Book design by Laurent Linn.
The text for this book was set in Clearface Gothic LT Std.
The illustrations for this book were rendered in acrylic paints on illustration board.

Text copyright © 2018 by Susan Verde.
Illustrations copyright © 2018 by John Parra.
All rights reserved. Published by Scholastic Inc., 557 Broadway, New York, NY 10012,
by arrangement with Simon & Schuster Children's Publishing Division,
a division of Simon & Schuster, Inc.
Printed in the U.S.A.

ISBN-13: 978-1-338-62147-1
ISBN-10: 1-338-62147-5

1 2 3 4 5 6 7 8 9 10   141   28 27 26 25 24 23 22 21 20 19

Scholastic Inc., 557 Broadway, New York, NY 10012

HEY, WALL

A STORY OF ART AND COMMUNITY

WRITTEN BY **Susan Verde**

ILLUSTRATED BY **John Parra**

SCHOLASTIC INC.

2

Hey, Wall!

You are **BIG**.
A city block **BIG**.
My city block.

3

Maybe once you were full of style,
but no one has taken care of you.
You are nothing to look at.
You are cold,
old,
empty.

4

5

Hey, Wall!

In the fall James and I skateboard past you as fast as we can on the way home from school.

6

In the winter the dirty snow
piles up in front of you.

No one shovels. Danny and her friends on the
block build their snowmen on other sidewalks.

In the spring Grandma Addy drinks iced tea on the stoop.
She talks of a time when our neighborhood was beautiful.

When you were beautiful!

8

In the summer the ice cream truck rolls by. We chase it to a spot far from you, where we let the ice cream melt on our tongues.

9

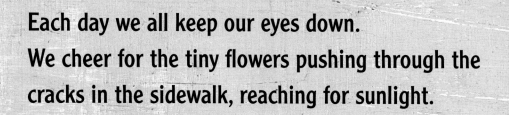

Each day we all keep our eyes down.
We cheer for the tiny flowers pushing through the
cracks in the sidewalk, reaching for sunlight.

No one looks up at you.
There is nothing to cheer for.
You are only lonely concrete.

Hey, Wall!

When we are inside with family,
friends, and neighbors,
there is love;
there is joy.

12

Can you smell what's cookin'?
We are eating together.
Can you hear the stories we share about
the way things used to be?
We are telling jokes,
belly laughing.

13

Can you hear our music?
We are salsa dancing.
We are hip-hopping.
We are dizzy from spinning.

14

We want to take it to the streets,
but you don't dance.
You don't laugh.
You don't share your stories.

15

Hey, Wall!

Guess what?

I'm ready to change *all* that.

17

I've got my pencil,
I've got my paints,
I've got my dreams.

Family Photos

18

I am a writer, a creator,
a game changer,
a *wall* changer.

19

James and Danny brought their sketches.
Grandma Addy brought her memories.
We've all brought our ideas and imagination.

We give you one last look,
and then we begin.

21

I call to my family, my friends, my neighbors.
We stand right in front of you,
staring you down.

You are *our* wall now.

You've become our blank canvas.

Your cracks and bumps and rough edges are our clean slate.

23

Up on ladders
and way down low.
Soon we have filled you with colors,
creations, energy.

You are stone but you don't have to be *hard*.

24

25

Hey, Wall!

Look at you now.
You are beautiful!

Now you tell the *real* story of *us*.

And together *we* are somethin' to see!

Angel

27

28

29

A Note from the Author

From as far back as I can remember, my life has been infused with art. I grew up in the heart of Greenwich Village in New York City and was fortunate enough to visit galleries and museums with my parents and on school trips. But it wasn't just within those buildings that I experienced art. With every subway ride I saw bubble letters and people's "tags" or names written on the sides of trains. With every stroll in our neighborhood I saw walls covered in colorful images. Some I could decipher and some were abstract, but each felt important and intriguing, like a secret language. I was fascinated by how a wall could act as a canvas and how what was painted on that canvas made a neighborhood or city block seem like an outdoor museum.

In the fourth grade my class created a mural on our playground wall. We each chose an element of New York we wanted to paint and then went on field trips to see and sketch what we had chosen. I picked the Manhattan Bridge. From there we made a model in our classroom deciding where everything should go, and then we got to paint right on the wall! It was an amazing experience for me, not only because we as kids were in charge of the design and creation of this mural, but also because in the end we had transformed our playground. The mural made us feel proud and connected to each other and our school. People passing by always stopped and admired our work. It affected the entire neighborhood. I felt as though we had joined the ranks of the graffiti and street artists. That's when it really clicked for me that *kids* have the ability to effect change through art.

As artists like Keith Haring hit the scene, graffiti, street art, and mural painting became even more significant. Keith Haring had this bubbly and playful style, through which he communicated messages about the world around him. His famous Carmine Street pool mural was one of my favorites. It was big and bold with fishlike creatures and figures that were a style all his own. He also created murals that expressed more serious topics of the time.

There is a difference between graffiti and street art, and it is important to make the distinction. Graffiti came first and was typically word-based. Artists would write their "tags" or names in places illegally, but it was still a form of self-expression with its own unique style. Street art was influenced by graffiti, but is created in places where permission has been granted or the artist has been commissioned to paint. Street art makes use of more imagery and materials than graffiti. Both hold a significant place in the evolution of outdoor art and self-expression.

Today we have festivals that celebrate street art and wall mural painting, and a long list of artists who share their hopes, dreams, voices, and messages through this art form. There is the Bushwick Collective in Brooklyn and the Art Basel festival in Miami and more. There is even an eight-year-old, Lola the Illustrator, who is making her mark in the street art world through her murals.

Walls often separate and divide. When neglected they can appear lonely and sad, but art and artists have the power to change that. A blank wall can become a canvas that unites and transforms neighborhoods and communities. It can become a place for messages of hope and pride, filled with emotion and personality. Street art can make a wall come alive.

It was my desire to write a story that pays tribute to street art and artists. But I also wanted to honor *kids*: their ideas and creativity give them the power to turn the ordinary into the extraordinary. *Hey, Wall* is that story and I am so proud to tell it.

—S. V.

A Note from the Illustrator

I grew up in the early 80s in Southern California. One of my earliest memories is of seeing outdoor murals from the backseat of our old family car while on a road trip. My parents would travel with my two brothers and me, up and down the state freeways, taking us on scenic drives and extended family visits. On a number of occasions we passed directly through the downtown area of Los Angeles. There, near the iconic LA City Hall, I would see them: large-scale murals decorating the cityscape. They had wonderful compositions, from colorful Chicano and urban cultural scenes to interstellar planets with floating Greek columns, and even several huge portraits of individuals painted in striking realism. The murals were often located on walls next to freeways and bridge underpasses; thus they were known as the Freeway Murals, painted to celebrate the Olympic Games that came to Los Angeles in 1984. I was in awe of the work. I asked, "How could someone create something so big and so detailed, and so AMAZING?" Every trip I would search for more and more murals and art.

As I grew into a young adult I began to study art and art history. Teachers and professors introduced me to more mural works, from Italian and Greek frescos to many of my favorite Mexican muralists, especially Diego Rivera. I fell in love with the beauty, power, and history these works projected. Art the size of a city block has a wonderful and direct connection to its community. You do not have to visit a museum or an art gallery. Art murals are there for you to enjoy from the street. They become part of our lives and conversations. Today in each city I visit, from San Francisco and San Diego to New York and Miami, there is always art to see.

One of my favorite things about becoming a professional artist is that I get to meet other amazing artists, some of whom I have admired for a very long time. While I was teaching at the Carnegie Art Museum in Oxnard, California, I took my class on a field trip to visit the studio of Frank Romero, a famous Chicano muralist. When I met him, I told him how much I enjoyed his work. I made sure to say that I especially enjoyed his freeway mural in downtown Los Angeles that inspired me all those years ago.

Mural artists like Frank Romero, Diego Rivera, and many others influenced my art style. How I tell a story with images, how I create a connection between the viewer and the subject matter, how I inspire others with concept and design is what I was thinking of when I created the art for *Hey, Wall*. I hope you enjoy our story and will look out for public art in your own community. And I hope you will be inspired to create and share your own mural.

—J. P.

31

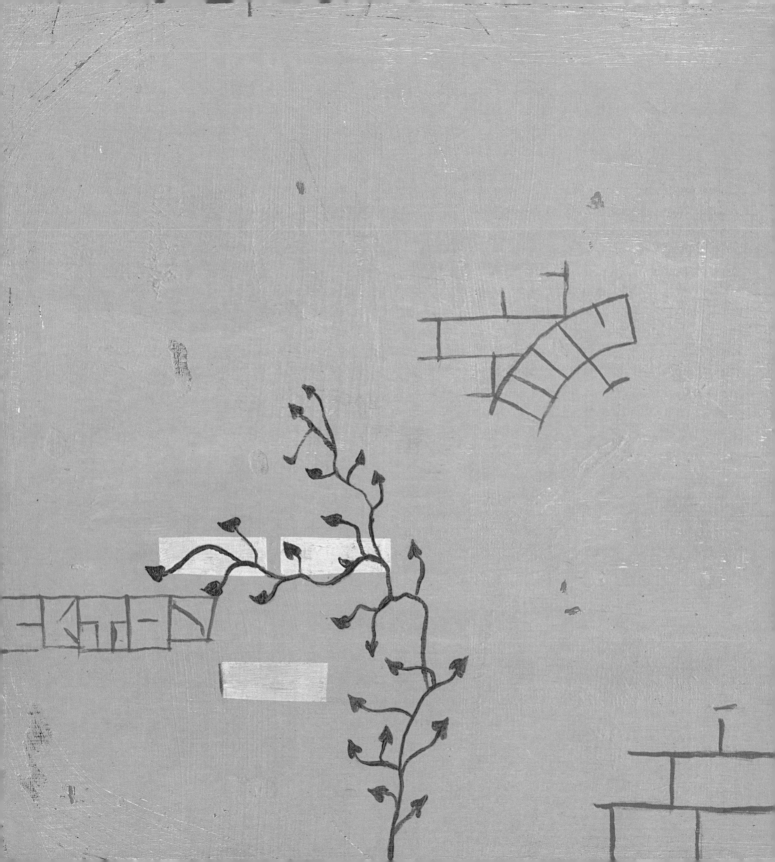